john wood and
paul harrison

MINIGRAPHS is a series of publications developed by ellipsis and Film and Video Umbrella devoted to contemporary artists from Britain who work primarily in the area of film and video. The series builds on a previous partnership in which ellipsis, as publishers, and Film and Video Umbrella, as project producers, joined forces to release a number of innovative digital art works, packaged as a CD-ROM with an accompanying book, on the label •••electric art. These new publications, while linking with 'Film and Video Artists on Tour', a programme of public presentations by each of the featured artists, are nevertheless designed to stand on their own, offering a concise and illuminating overview of the artists' influences and preoccupations and highlighting the growing interest in film and video within contemporary visual art.

We would like to thank the National Lottery through the Arts Council of England and London Film and Video Development Agency for their support of this initiative.

Tom Neville, •••ellipsis
Steven Bode, Film and Video Umbrella

john wood and paul harrison

with essays by charles esche and david batchelor

●●●ellipsis

First published 2000 by
●●●ellipsis
2 Rufus Street
London N1 6PE
www.ellipsis.com

A collaboration with Film and Video Umbrella, published to accompany the
Film and Video Umbrella touring project 'Film and Video Artists on Tour'

This publication was supported by the National Lottery through the Arts
Council of England, and received additional funding from the University of
Wolverhampton

film and video umbrella

ISBN 1 84166 026 4
Design by Claudia Schenk
Printed and bound in Spain by Gráficas Varona

●●●ellipsis is a trademark of Ellipsis London Limited

British Library Cataloguing in Publication Data: a CIP record for this
publication is available from the British Library

For a copy of the Ellipsis catalogue or information on special quantity
orders of Ellipsis books please contact sales on
020 7739 3157 or sales@ellipsis.co.uk

contents

2002-599

Some of this starts at school. As I child in the 1970s, I used to wait with avid expectation for the days after New Year. On the 3rd or 4th of January, the series of Royal Institution Christmas Lectures for Children and Young People would start at around 10.30 am on BBC1 television. The talks might range from 'how gravity works' to 'space exploration in the next century', but it was less the subject of the series than the method of delivery that thrilled me. Here was a scientist sharing a secret knowledge about the future that we children were going to inherit. What's more, he (they were always men in the 1970s) was doing it in a big academic lecture hall and making a mess – playing about with unlikely combinations of huge test tubes, kid-size harnesses and oxyacetylene torches to concoct elaborate, television-scale experiments. In fact, it was these experiments that really caught my imagination. Every year, the same technician would set them up, keep them going, take care of the panicking lecturer when the bench caught fire or he dropped the test tube. He even chose which children would be led down from the audience to show us what happens when water evaporates or the sun goes supernova. The technician was, I think, called Alfred: he had lots of white hair, a lab coat and I really wanted his job.

I mention all this because something of the same fascination clings to the work of John Wood and Paul Harrison. Their collaborative work invokes the memory of the 1970s and not just in its art-historical references to Bruce Nauman or Chris Burden. Their work also has the air of those Royal Institution lectures, as these two serious men present their activities and interim conclusions to a respectful though slightly bemused public. Like the lecturers of my youth, Wood and Harrison never quite manage to completely suppress a smile and that slight twinkle in the eye that tells us they know what we are thinking. It has something of the atmosphere of the old BBC, in fact – a little po-faced, a little 'make do and mend', but always aspirational for its viewers. In fact, just the kind of face to ensure that the squeals of delight are all the louder when things seem to go wrong or the protagonist does not appear to be completely in control.

'nohow on'

charles esche

OPPOSITE 'Two Wall Sections'

Screen 1: '3 Legged', 1996
Viewed on a monitor, the two artists are tied together at the ankle and confined within a simple wooden shelter open on one side. Facing them, an automatic tennis server oscillates across the foreground, shooting balls out at intervals. It looks like a home-made cannon and delivers its missiles with surprising force. The two men try to avoid the balls – tripping, falling, sliding and pushing each other around. The motor of the tennis server is the only constant sound, switching up an octave whenever it is about to shoot. The whole sequence lasts three tense minutes. John gets hit a lot more than Paul and we hear his groans. Towards the end, exhausted, they work out that all they have to do is duck. Just after this, the server exhausts its supply of balls and starts firing blanks. John looks at the camera and thus the viewer. He lets us in on his relief while Paul looks away, catching his breath. The two of them then sit, still bound, as far away from each other as they can manage. End.

When two men put themselves through this sort of test, we think less of scientific experiments than about army exercises, teamwork, the pain threshold and mateship forged through struggle. This is very male territory, but located where instinct and spirit count for more than the disembodied intellect. Does it demand comment, when men show their emotions and fallabilities in this way? In one sense it does, because, even as artists, men are often assumed, for a complex tangle of reasons, to be less willing to expose their private failings. Wood and Harrison expose not just their bodies' vulnerability but something more hidden, an orchestrated emotional frailty as well as a kind of mutual dependence that would be destroyed if articulated in words. It's very male, very silent and very touching.

Occasionally, as in '3 Legged', the relationship between the two protagonists comes even further to the fore. In earlier pieces such as 'Crossover (I miss you)' and 'Board' the two mimic each other's actions, moving simultaneously across, underneath or around a found object or group of objects such as a table and two chairs. The simplicity of the set-ups prefigures all of their later work with more abstract structures but the closeness of contact between the two is something less detectable in subsequent work. That this close proximity is based on professional trust rather than personal intimacy is significant because it places the emphasis of the action not on the body as a presence but as an active agent. Expression through action in ways that might recall Jackson Pollock as much as modern dance.

The choreography of movements in both these works and later pieces such as 'Two Wall Sections' suggests that it is possible to recognise their relationship to contemporary dance, or, at least and because of the knot of negative theatrical associations that dance tied itself into in the 1990s, to the movement of bodies through space. This brings it close to the initial interests of Bruce Nauman, an artist of much influence not only on Wood and Harrison but on so many young contemporary artists. In a 1970 interview with Willoughby Sharp, Nauman explained his relationship to the body and movement:

> The first time I really talked to anybody about body
> awareness was in the summer of 1968. Meredith Monk was
> in San Francisco. She had thought about or seen some of my
> work and recognised it ... An awareness of yourself comes
> from a certain amount of activity and you can't get it from
> just thinking about yourself ... The films and some of the
> pieces I did after that for videotapes were specifically about
> doing exercises in balance. I thought of them as dance
> problems without being a dancer.[1]

In this interview, Nauman is clearly picking up on the theoretical writings of Maurice Merleau-Ponty, a theorist whose work serves as a useful illumination of possible meaning in much performance and video art from the 1960s onwards. In Merleau-Ponty's *Phenomenology of Perception*, he writes about 'the body image' as having a distinct relationship to space:

> The body image is dynamic, which means that my body
> appears to me as an attitude directed to a certain existing or
> possible task ... (not) a spatiality of position but a spatiality
> of situation ... The body image is finally a way of stating
> that my body is in-the-world ... It is clearly in action that the
> spatiality of our body is brought into being.[2]

As we have seen, for Wood and Harrison this idea of working through a task or action is central to their practice. They then take the identified action through to an absurd, if logical, conclusion in order to find out what happens if the movement is tested to destruction. So, as a conclusion to many of the 'performances', we find not a crescendo of activity but exhaustion, collapse and failure, or its analogue in endless video-loop repetition.

'3 Legged'

Screen 2: 'Device', 1996

Viewed on a monitor, we see six vignettes of a body under command. The space is white, the objects white or grey. The series opens with a white screen. We wait an extended period until a crash mat falls from above into the line of sight of the camera. A man, John Wood, is parcelled to it with string. He lands smack on the floor, no movement afterwards, just wait and fade. The second object/body construct is a steady ascension on a cylindrical inflatable confined within a narrow wooden channel; the third suspends the figure in mid-dive, the diving board pulled back to complete the composition. The fourth has John standing at the bottom of a steep constructed slope. Fixed to his feet, wooden blocks serve as risers as he carries his own staircase up the slope to rest still at the top. The fifth places him on a conveyor belt, his body stretched out to its limits in either direction. Lastly, a semi-circular curved structure rolls through 180 degrees to crash into a wall at the absolute edge of the monitor screen.

It is difficult for us, as viewers, to avoid observing performances like 'Device' or the darker 'Volunteer' as a laboratory technician might watch the activities of a creature responding to specific stimuli and controlled situations. Of course, we always remain conscious of the fact that the artists control the initial proposition and afterwards choose to become their own material in the experiment, but the evidence on the screen suggests some level of external control or even coercion from one partner on another. It is almost as if the works are designed to test out the tolerance of an individual's psychology when put under command and physical constraint. 'Volunteer' complicates matters further by engaging the test situation with intimations of external conditions: for instance, the arm raised in assent dragged up by a rope operated off-screen, or the slow motion, rope-controlled fall down a flight of stairs. Both hint at a possible narrative that extends the experiment into the area of personal and perhaps social control. Here lies an indication of a relationship to minimal theatre that will be extended later.

For now, it is the more sinister aspect of 'Volunteer' that is of interest, something that is also evident in 'Harry Houdini (There's no escape that I can see)'. In both these works, the constrictions of the screen as a cage for the image are manipulated to the full. 'Harry Houdini' traps one of the artists inside a transparent container half-filled with water. As the waterline rotates inexplicably through 360 degrees, the trapped figure struggles, successfully, to keep his head above water. The sequence ends when the movement comes to rest where it began, the figure once again seated, head and shoulders clear and with no change to his initial situation. The rotation then loops again. The sheer pointlessness of this strategy for survival is laid bare by this return to a state of immobility, something that is shared with many other cyclical sequences in their work. Of course, as we shall see with reference to the work of Samuel Beckett, Bruce Nauman, Yvonne Rainer and others, this very repetitiveness is partly the point of Wood and Harrison's work. The subject of their investigations is as much the forlornness and compulsion of activity for its own sake as a study of their bodies and the psychology of their relationship. This repetition, this 'going on', iterated through looped projections and video installations, is fundamental to the work. It brings coherence to the many different sequences and links us, as viewers and individual subjects, to the otherwise hermetic quality of the experiments, drawing us in by recalling our own ambivalence to the purpose of activity while nevertheless remaining active.

On one level, then, 'Volunteer', 'Device' and related works can be defined as investigations of these actions. Yet we must not ignore the very closely related investigation of the body itself. Paul Valéry, the Symbolist poet and critic, brings action and the body beautifully together in an extract from his notebooks:

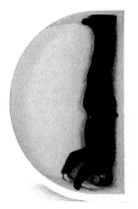

'Device'

> When I look at a living thing, what I see and what first
> occupies my attention is this mass, all of a piece, which
> moves, bends, runs, jumps, flies or swims; which howls,
> speaks, sings, performs in many acts, takes on many
> appearances, assumes a multiplicity of selves, wreaks its
> havoc, does its work, in an environment which accepts it and
> from which it is inseparable. This thing, with its
> discontinuous activity, its spontaneous movements springing
> suddenly from a state of immobility to which they always
> return, is curiously contrived: we note that the visible organs
> of propulsion, legs, feet, wings, occupy a considerable part of
> the creature's total bulk; we discover later on that the rest of
> its volume is made up of organs of internal work, some of
> whose outward effects we have witnessed. It would seem as
> though the creature's whole span were the effect of the work,
> as though its entire production, visible or not, were
> expended in feeding the insatiable consumer of matter that
> the creature is.[3]

Valéry continues this text by suggesting that, in fact, the body is not the self-sufficient organism described here, or, at least, that there are other bodies perceived in different ways as something that 'belongs to us', or 'that others see', or 'that is reduced to its parts and pieces', and finally, one that is 'an indivisible and unknowable object'. These definitions of the body turn on the quality of perception that is applied and they reverberate in Wood and Harrison's work in the way their roles slip from experimenter to experimentee, between practicing artist and bodily subject. Within this, their pairing as two distinct, identifiable figures as well as collaborating partners is significant. Each observes, modifies and manipulates the other, at times literally in a work like 'Headstand'. The presence of another figure in many of the works also serves to complicate the viewers' relationship to the performance. There is already a primary observer and the loop of subject and object can be closed without any recourse to an external viewer. So our role as the 'audience' becomes even more pointedly voyeuristic, looking in from the outside on to games with their own logic between the two of them. This isn't just about bodies but (as always) about psychological tests of friendship and trust.

Screen 3: 'Obstacle Course', 1999
Gallery installation with video monitors. Six human-scale structures reminiscent of models for gymnasium equipment are placed in a space or series of connected rooms. The layout suggests a cycle of exercises, perhaps a competitive course. The soundtrack supplies the narrative, tracking the movements of an unseen athlete as he negotiates each obstacle in turn. A single monitor in or on each structure is mostly blank, only coming to life when the figure passes its position on the circuit. Then, for a moment, Paul Harrison appears, in close-up and life size in the frame of the monitor. The course is lapped a number of times at different speeds as Harrison tires or pushes himself harder. Almost imperceptibly, it loops, so the runner keeps on running, keeps on tiring, keeps on picking himself up and starting again.

'Obstacle Course' is about effort expended and time passing. 'Nohow on', to quote Beckett as the master of works that record 'the passage of time or … the refusal of time to pass'.[4] Indeed, we cannot end without a consideration of Samuel Beckett. Performance art begins where he stops; except, of course, his characters never begin nor end but simply keep on keeping on. That is the beauty in his work – and its melancholy. So, the first time you see certain sequences in 'Volunteer' you may laugh: John suspended alongside a chair; both then raised in parallel about 1 metre from the floor; John pulled through a narrow white channel, looking uncomfortable but uncomplaining. The second time you see or think about it, the piece changes. The humour, which was never laugh-out-loud funny, fades away to be replaced by recollections of other misfortunates, perhaps Lucky in *Waiting for Godot*, the chained slave who thought himself dependent on his master for his survival. This is perhaps most forcibly felt in the section where John tries to leap into the air only to be pulled down – a sprawling figure on the floor – by the rope round his ankles. At this point, your thoughts might turn to systemic abuses of power and people's (in)voluntarily complicity in such situations. Partly, you would be justified because such seriousness is never that far away from Wood and Harrison's work, but the language feels imposed from another discourse, one that the artists know but do not labour. Care is essential however, as meaning in the late 1990s is a tricky matter. Let us remind ourselves of Beckett, again.

> Hamm: We're not beginning to ...... to ...... mean something?
> Clov: Mean something! You and I mean something! Ah, that's a good one.[5]

Perhaps, and again returning to the 1970s, the connection between Beckett and Wood and Harrison is illuminated more by the dancer and choreographer Yvonne Rainer's description of her own working process at the time of the *Continuous Project* series of works:

> There are primary, secondary and tertiary performances. Primary performance is what we are already doing – original material. Most performance is secondary, i.e. performing someone else's material in a style approximating the original or working in a known style or 'genre' ... I want our spoken stuff to be tertiary – someone else's material, or material that has actually previously been brought into existence (via media or live), as though it is one's own, but in a style completely different from or inappropriate to the original ... It all adds up to a kind of irony that has always fascinated me ... I feel that the tension is produced from not knowing

whether someone is reciting or saying something – pushes a performance back and forth 'in and out of warp'. The days of thwarted expectation are over. Warping is the ticket!

Beckett warped? In and out between the great existential questions and Keystone Cops humour? Perhaps it's the deadpan earnestness of the expressions on both the artists' faces that makes the reference seem just about appropriate. Of perhaps it is the already warped nature of Beckett himself. In the central scene in Beckett's one foray into film (called, simply enough, *Film*), a elderly man attempts to hide from the world. First the animals must go. He picks up the cat and puts it out of the room. Turning, he picks up the dog, a strange miniature smaller than the cat, and opens the door. The cat rushes back in. He chases the cat, picks it up, opens the door, and the dog runs in. This loops around 16 times until the man, slowed and tiring, finally succeeds in isolating himself. Classic slapstick, but only later, as the camera finally moves round to show his face for the first time, do we realise who the distressed, hunched figure is. Buster Keaton, 25 years after his silent-movie heyday, looking older but no sadder than his lost innocent character of 1927. Beckett himself, giving instructions for the cat and dog scene, said, 'Expressions of this episode … should be as precisely styled as possible'.7

Wood and Harrison understand that better than many of their contemporaries. In work which is celebrated for its lightness, the slightest archness in the presentation can cause the whole edifice of warped meaning and underdone humour to fall apart. To avoid it, the structures and devices with which they populate their works have to be just as 'precisely styled' as the performance. Stripped to the bone, the structures just give sufficient clue as to their function to make sense of the piece.

Screen 4: 'Boat', 1994
On monitor or projection, the two artists start rocking a curved, hull-like form open at one side. The structure is tightly contained within the limits of the recorded image, its vertical position exactly aligning with the edge of the monitor or projection. The 'boat' itself is yellow like a Cornish fishing vessel. As the rocking accelerates, the two figures change position frequently to keep the momentum going and to increase the angle of incidence. They cross over, move from side to side, rescue themselves from overbalancing, in attempted collaboration. It ends, as these things must, in going one step too far. The boat, at its highest point, refuses to swing down and back into the centre of the image. Instead, it escapes gravity and topples over on to its back. Just as

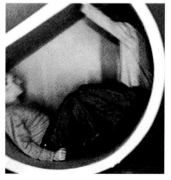
'Boat'

it falls out of sight, the screen cuts to the left to catch the now-doomed boat with its two occupants smacking loudly into the solid wood of its upended base. Pause a while and then end.

The smack into the ground is actually one of the recurring leitmotifs in Wood and Harrison's work. In quite a literal way, it keeps it down to earth or, in Beckett's words, a 'matter of fundamental sounds (no joke intended) made as fully as possible'.[8] 'Boat' is what it is, an elaborate children's game taken too far. The fundamental smack at the end becomes a puncturing of certain pretensions on behalf of artists, scientists and the approving audience. We are common men, they seem to be saying, and we play games and make mistakes like the rest of you. Meaning in the work is not found in the artists' pain and suffering, as might be true of Chris Burden or Carolee Schneemann. Instead, it lies in the construction and drama of the scenario itself, in 'Boat' as a knowingly childish moral tale in which no good comes to those who go that little bit too far. The morality here is as much Edward Lear as Samuel Beckett, perhaps because it is more difficult to explore such an issue today than it was even through the absurd mundanity of Beckett. Because of this lack of a larger moral framework, Wood and Harrison seem to suggest that we only have empirical science and childish naivete to guide some of our most significant decisions. Neither is up to the job, of course, so we end up with the modest cruelty of 'Volunteer' and the slapstick catastrophe of 'Boat'. These are presented, without any particular sadness, as the poles of possible expression through the body. It is through the constant persistence of their experiments and demonstrations that some form of change or development is suggested. Otherwise we have the pleasurable pointlessness of discovering much and learning very little. So the end result of these serious, deadpan tasks, minimally created, is not very worthy at all. Rather, it is frivolous in the best and most constructive sense. 'Nohow on' and always remember to laugh sometimes.

1 Willoughby Sharp, 'Bruce Nauman', *Avalanche*, winter 1971, quoted in *Outside the Frame – Performance and the Object*, Cleveland Centre for Contemporary Art, 1994

2 Maurice Merleau-Ponty, *Phenomenology of Perception*, trans. Colin Smith, Routledge and Kegan Paul, London, 1962, quoted in Henry M Sayre, *The Object of Performance: The American Avant-Garde Since 1970*, University of Chicago Press, 1989

3 Paul Valéry, 'Some Simple Reflections on the Body' in *Fragments for a History of the Human Body*, Zone Books, New York, 1989 p 395

4 Samuel Beckett, *Worstward Ho*, Grove, New York, 1981, p 58

5 Samuel Beckett, *Endgame followed by Act without Words*, Faber & Faber, London, 1958 p 45

6 Yvonne Rainer, quoted in Henry M Sayre, *The Object of Performance: The American Avant-Garde Since 1970*.

7 *Film* by Samuel Beckett, complete scenario, illustrations and production shots, Faber and Faber, London 1972, pp 57-60

8 Martin Esslin (ed.), *Samuel Beckett, A collection of Critical Essays*, Prentice-Hall, New Jersey, 1965

crossover (i miss you)

A sequence of movements involving two figures and a table.
1 minute/VHS/1993

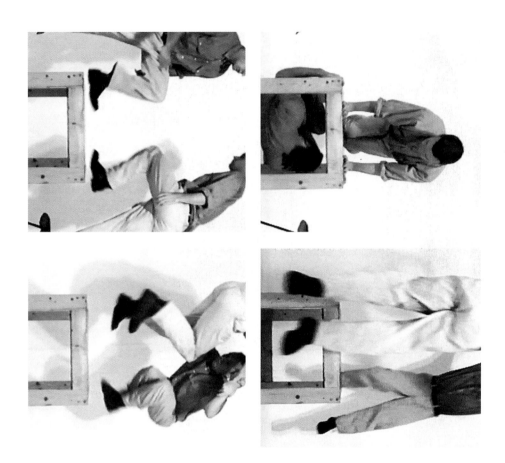

question and answer

'Crossover (I miss you)' is interrupted by a telephone ringing.
1 minute 15 seconds/VHS/1993

table 2

Two figures jump on to a table.
20 seconds/S-VHS/1993

board

Two figures manipulate a board across a space.
3 minutes/S-VHS/1993

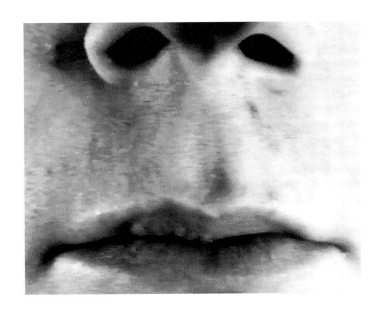

breathe

A figure exhales after one minute.
1:00 min/S-VHS/1993

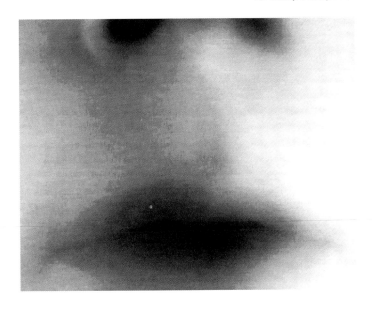

harry houdini (there's no escape that i can see)

A figure moves within a box (half filled with water) that rotates 360°.
1 minute 45 seconds/Hi8/1994
Funded by South West Arts

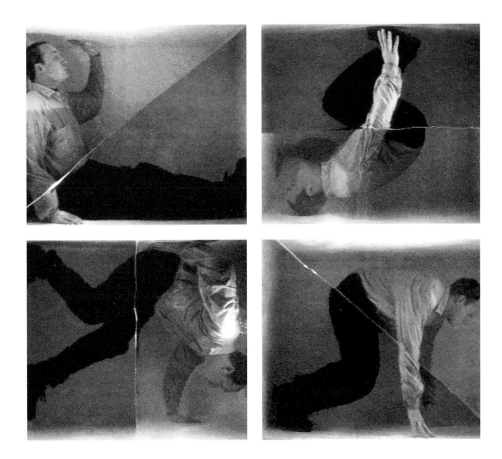

headstand

Figure 1 stands in a box that is inverted by figure 2.
1 minute/Hi8/1995

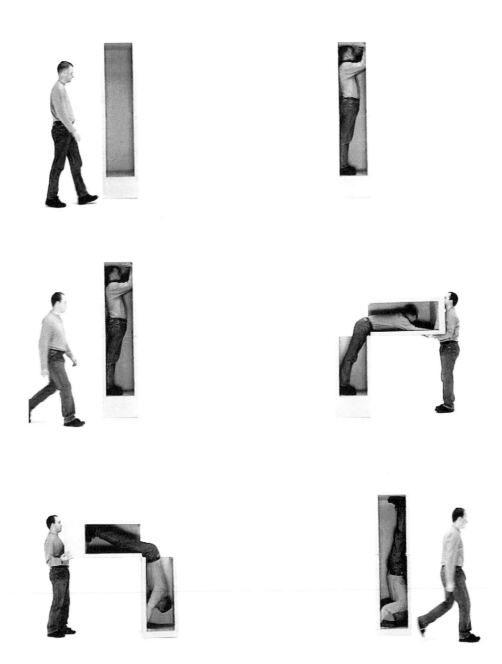

plinth

A figure climbs and stands on top of a plinth.
30 seconds/Hi8/1995

boat

Two figures rock a cross-section of a boat backwards and forwards.
1 minute 45 seconds/U-Matic/1994
Funded by Film and Video Umbrella/West Midlands Arts

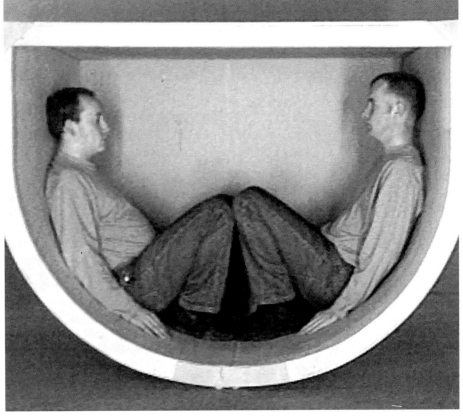

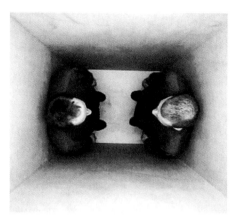 

shaft

Figure 1 climbs on to the shoulders of figure 2 and switches the camera off.
1 minute 10 seconds/Hi8/1995

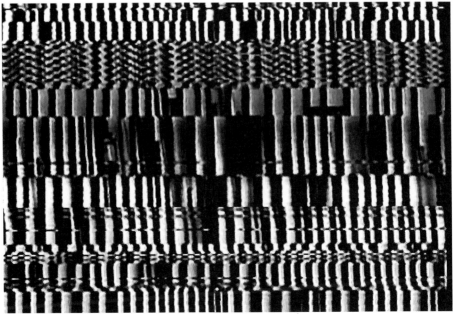

device

Six devices enable a figure to move in six directions across the screen.
3 minutes/Beta/1996
Commissioned by BBC2 and the Arts Council of England

six boxes (life size)

A figure interacts with six different boxes.
4 minutes/miniDV/1997
Funded by Film and Video Umbrella /West Midlands Arts

 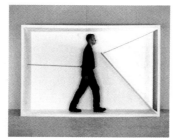 

october 97

A figure interacts with thirteen different objects.
8 minutes/Beta/1997
Commissioned by Werkleitz Gesellschaft (European Media Artist in Residence Exchange)

3 legged

Two figures try to avoid being hit by tennis balls fired from a machine.
3 minutes/Hi8/1996

untitled 1996

Tennis balls are fired through a wall at a man standing in water.
7 minutes/Hi8/1996

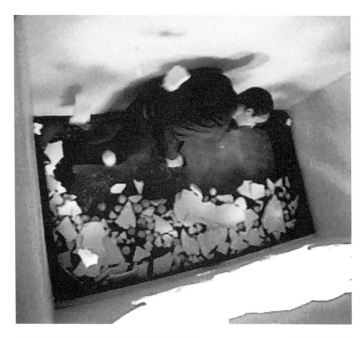

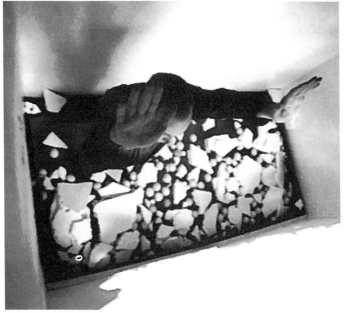

upside down

The camera turns 180°.
1 minute 40 seconds/miniDv/1998
Supported by The National Lottery through the Arts Council of England

50 john wood and paul harrison

two wall sections

Figure 1 holds figure 2 against a wall.
1 minute/DV/1998
Supported by The National Lottery through the Arts Council of England

Because you're waiting for someone
Because you've seen something
Because you're listening
Because you're thinking
Because it's your job
Because you don't know where you are
Because you're trying not to fall over
Because you've been told to
Because you don't want to move
Because you can't move
Because you want to be seen
Because you don't want to be seen
To have your photo taken

12 reasons to stand somewhere

A figure stands against a wall (subtitled).
1 minute 10 seconds/DV/1998

volunteer

A figure is manipulated via a rope leading off screen.
6 minutes/miniDV/1998

boat 2

A figure sits in a boat that is rotated 180°.
A figure climbs over a boat that is rotated 180°.
3 minutes/miniDV/2000

Art is often continued by creatively missing the point of earlier art. Minimalism, the operational grammar of so much art of the last 35 years, has had its various points missed perhaps more consistently and comprehensively than any other 'movement' of the 20th century. This is cause for general celebration, of course, except perhaps among minimalism's purists who, having missed the point just as much as anyone else, then missed the point that they had missed the point. The real legacy of minimalism is a bestiary, a hall of mirrors, the Hell rather than the Heaven of a Bosch altarpiece. Art is continued by being continuously corrupted, and minimalism has been continued in any number of ways. For many, the apparent emptiness of minimalist form has been something to be appropriated and filled in. (It doesn't matter whether minimalist form can properly be described as 'empty'; it's enough that it can be made to appear so under certain circumstances.) The minimalist box has become the perfect container for all sorts of foreign bodies – actual bodies, virtual bodies, animal, vegetable or mineral bodies. In John Wood and Paul Harrison's videos, it is as if the generic, geometric, blank, white container – not-quite-sculpture and not-yet-architecture, and not any actual specific object – has been broken-into, squatted and used to host an unofficial slow-motion party. It's a strange party, to be sure, with strange dancing and strange drugs, but it's a party in the sense of something improper and unlicensed going on. At least, that is how it appears …

In 1961 Robert Morris made a 2-foot by 2-foot by 8-foot plywood 'column'. It was painted pale grey and placed on its own in the centre of a stage. The audience watched it stand there for three-and-a-half minutes until suddenly it toppled over, landed on its side and rested there for a further three-and-a-half minutes. The object had been set in motion by a wire which the artist had pulled from the wings, although Morris had intended to stand inside the hollow form and knock it over with his own body-weight. When he tried this in rehearsal, however, Morris split his head open as the box hit the ground. (Imagine a horizontal pale grey 2-foot by 2-foot by 8-foot box with a small pool of crimson blood seeping out of one end.) This anecdote is a tiny footnote in the history of minimalism but it is a useful reminder that the human body and some sense of performance was literally and not just philosophically connected with minimalism; it indicates that artists such as Morris and Nauman, and perhaps also Judd, Andre, Flavin and LeWitt, were open to the comic possibilities of geometry; and it suggests that the work of Wood and Harrison enacts a kind of return of these often repressed characteristics of the genre. That is, if Wood and Harrison have continued minimalism by corrupting it, it is a corruption that has come from within rather than one visited from without.

But whose minimalism is being corrupted? Not any actual work made by one of a few North American artists during the 1960s. Rather the myth of minimalism as it has been propagated and handed down, more by art historians and interior designers than by artists. This mythical minimalism is also the mythical 'white cube' of a mythical modernism. It never actually existed (minimalism was rarely simply white or simply cubic), but it had to be brought into being in order then to be ritually put to the sword. Wood and Harrison's micro-dramas are enacted in such a white cube, a 'pure' and therefore unreal space which nevertheless has had a very real effect on the Western cultural imagination. Whiteness, of course, has long been the locus of virtue and purity in the West. Its recent history includes neo-classicism and the rhetoric of architecture from Adolph Loos and Le Corbusier to the interior designs of John Pawson and Claudio Silvestrin. The deconstruction of whiteness, in the hands of Joseph Conrad and Herman Melville, is a kind of parallel text to the writings of Winkelmann and Walter Pater, but it is in the work of Mikhail Bakhtin that the 20th century found its most brilliant critic of whiteness and, not coincidentally, analyst of corruption. Bakhtin's *Rabelais and his World* is largely a discussion of the grotesque imagery in Rabelais' work, but it is also easy to read as an assault on the 'classicism' of Stalinist Socialist Realism. For Bakhtin, this classical form is above all a self-contained unity, a body or form which is finite, closed and individuated. It is cut off from all around it, and anything that 'protrudes, bulges, sprouts, or branches off' is carefully 'eliminated, hidden or moderated'. This body has no orifices, and therefore nothing can enter it or be expelled from it. It is impenetrable. It cannot mutate or merge with anything beyond its boundaries. It has no relationship with the rest of the world and it has no inner life. This body is ultra-apolline: the elimination of all contingency and uncertainty. This imagery of an impenetrable, uninfectable whiteness is counterposed by Bakhtin with the strikingly visceral and dionysiac vision of the medieval body, a body which is constantly in the process of filling itself up and emptying itself out, of gorging and vomiting. It is all orifices and motions, constantly blending with other bodies and the world, mutating and becoming fluid. Bakhtin's universe is an opposition of the pure and clean and static (which is dead) and the impure and dirty and dynamic (which is living); it is also an opposition of the official and the popular, exclusivity and vulgarity, piety and laughter. His Carnival is the corruption of the official and the formal by the unofficial and improvised; it is a dethroning of the fixed by the mobile; and thus it is a renewal of life.

Bakhtin's imagery is both beautiful and desperate; his

falling over

david batchelor

Carnival is gorgeous but out of reach. Nevertheless, his imagery still plays on the imagination and it is played out in aspects of minimalism, pop art and performance. And, arguably, it is replayed by Wood and Harrison in works such as 'Device', '3 Legged', and '6 Boxes', albeit in a far more homely and domesticated manner. The impenetrable whiteness of their white cube appears to fill nothing more grand than the plastic casing of a television monitor; their bodily interventions don't mess up the space too much. Although they do occasionally rattle the box and reveal some dodgy carpentry, they tend more often to rattle themselves. They mess up their clothes a little in the process. Their struggles are not epic or heroic, and although their comedy is occasionally painful, for the most part they enact history as farce. Their corruption is a small downfall from no great height, with minor degradation and superficial bruising. It leaves a residue, nonetheless. The residue is the possibility that every hermetic architectural or artistic white cube we pass by might have a choreographed punchup going on inside. It also leaves behind the question as to why these days the Fall is a subject better suited to comedy than tragedy. For Baudelaire, the laughter that follows seeing someone slip on a banana skin is a complex laughter, both comic and tragic; it is both the pleasure that is never far from someone else's misfortune, and the pain of humanity's collective fall from grace. For Wood and Harrison, the Fall is an everyday occurance, repeated like an expressionless habit of everyday life: get up, get dressed, fall over, get up, etc, etc. It is hardly a catastrophe. There are no catastrophes, just a little discomfort here and there. And just as there are no catastrophes, nor are there any great victories worthy of being remembered for more than a couple of minutes after the event. It's a small world with small gains and small losses. Somehow that's funny, but it's also frustrating. The frustration registered in Wood and Harrison's work is not that of the dispossessed, as there is little sign of real fear or anger. Rather theirs is the frustration of knowing nothing much will happen today, just as it didn't yesterday or the day before. It is the frustration of knowing that the big catastrophes and the big victories will happen in another country to other people who we don't recognise and won't meet. None of this is necessarily true, of course, but sometimes art can make it feel that way, because in art the grand statement seems an increasingly remote possibility.

This perhaps is the real problem with minimalism: it is exhausted and in that sense truly empty, but somehow it remains an inescapable framework for so much contemporary art. And this may be why it all feels so frustrating, so repetitive and, occasionally, so funny. Minimalism is to Wood and Harrison something like what religion was to Dr. Aziz in Salman Rushdie's *Midnight's Children*: he is caught (also after cracking his head open on a hard surface) in a state of incomplete apostacy, and he is left 'no longer praying to a god in whom he could not entirely disbelieve'.

obstacle course

A running man races to negotiate a circuit of large
sculptural obstacles.

circular walk

A pair of feet tread the outline of a circle.

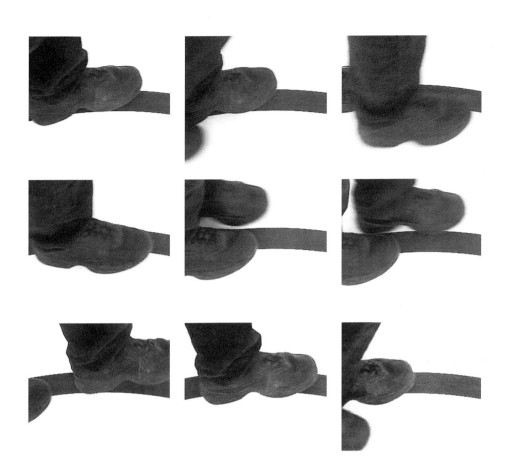

flood

A figure lying on the floor is gradually surrounded by blue liquid

pavement

Multiple pairs of feet walk across an elevated pavement.

 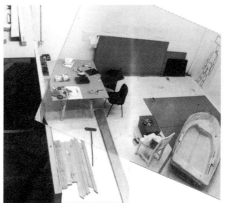

studio

john wood and paul harrison 77

drawings

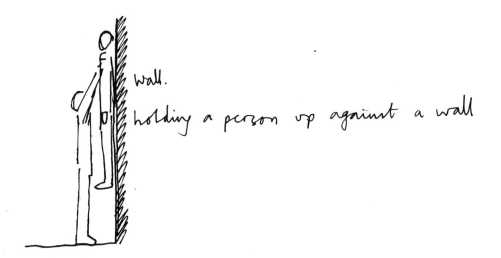

wall.

holding a person up against a wall

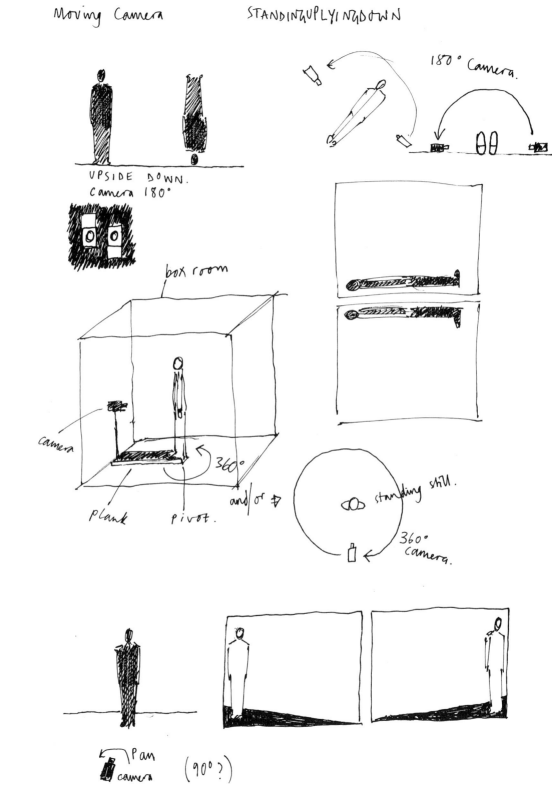

Moving Camera STANDINGUPLYINGDOWN

180° Camera.

UPSIDE DOWN.
Camera 180°

box room

camera

plank pivot.

360°

and/or ⊕

standing still.

360°
camera.

Pan
camera (90°?)

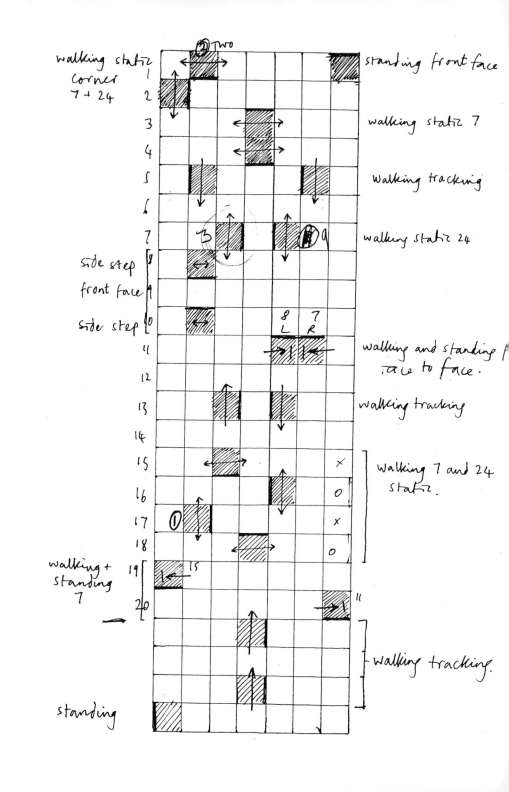

two

walking static
corner
7 + 24

1
2
3
4
5
6
7

side step
front face
side step

8
9
10
11
12
13
14
15
16
17
18

walking +
standing
7

19
20

standing

standing front face

walking static 7

walking tracking

walking static 24

walking and standing
face to face.

walking tracking

walking 7 and 24
static.

8   7
L   R

15

11

walking tracking.

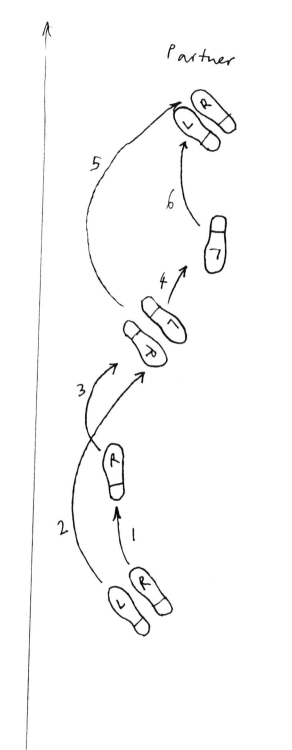

Partner

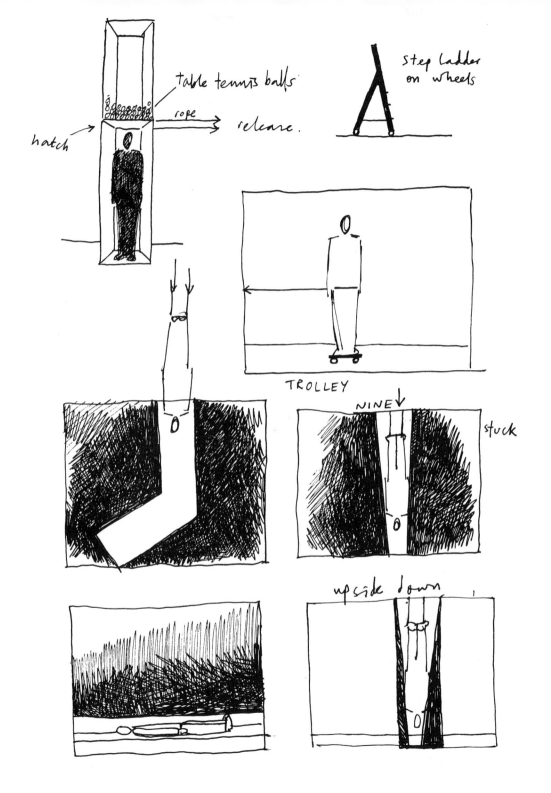

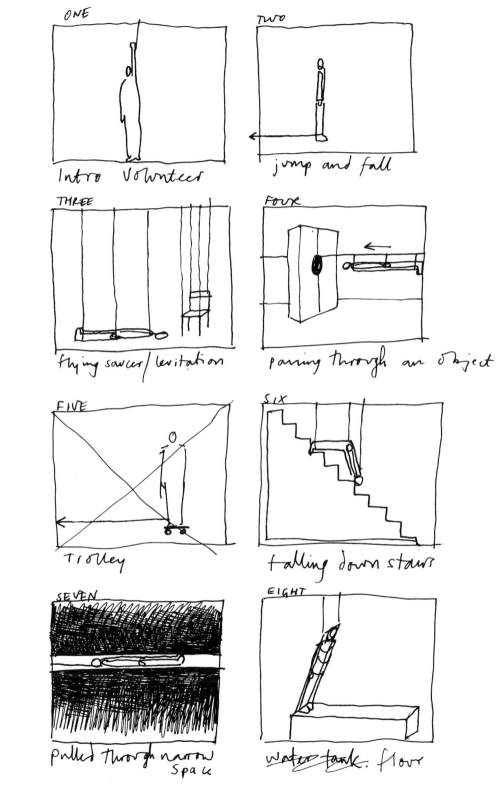

ONE

Intro Volunteer

TWO

jump and fall

THREE

flying saucer/levitation

FOUR

passing through an object

FIVE

Trolley

SIX

falling down stairs

SEVEN

pulled through narrow space

EIGHT

~~water tank.~~ floor

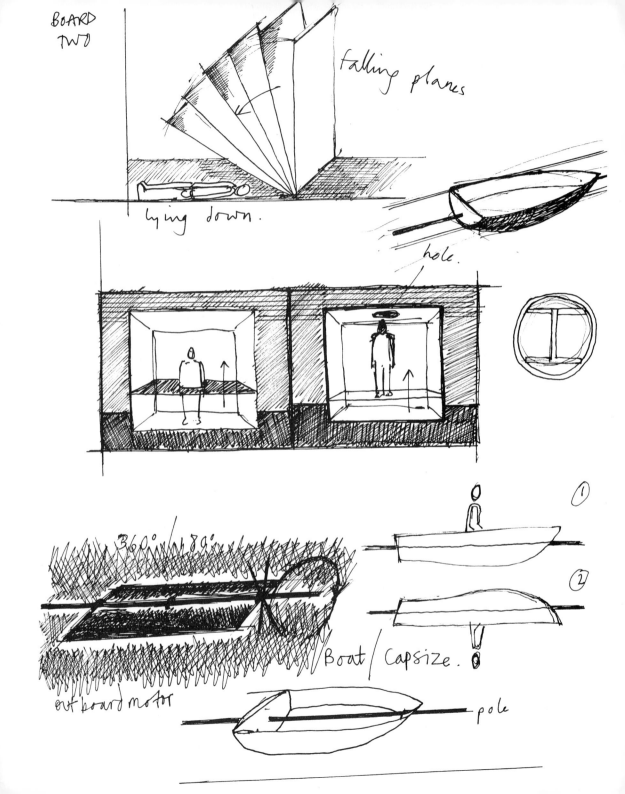

BOARD TWO

falling planes

lying down.

hole.

360° 180°

outboard motor

Boat / Capsize.

pole

①

②

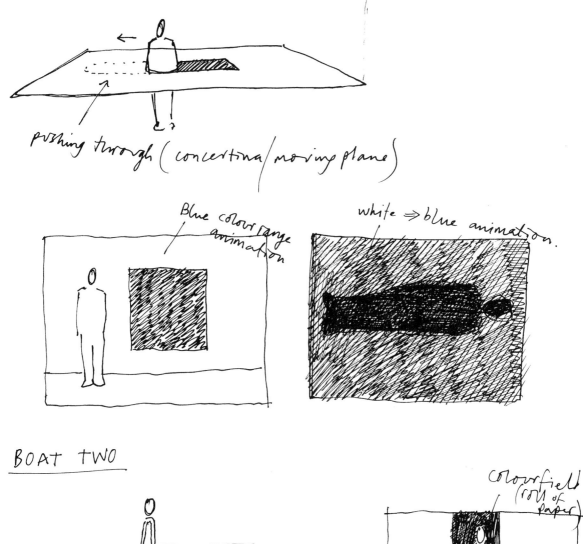

pushing through (concertina/moving plane)

Blue colourange animation

white ⇒ blue animation.

BOAT TWO

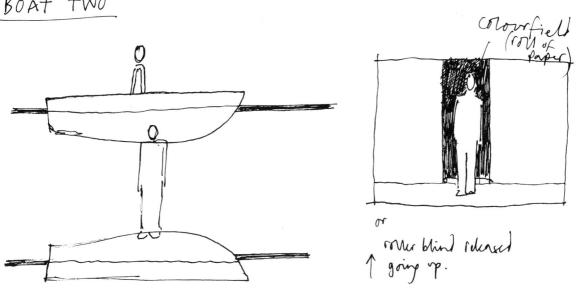

colourfield (roll of paper)

or

↑ roller blind released going up.

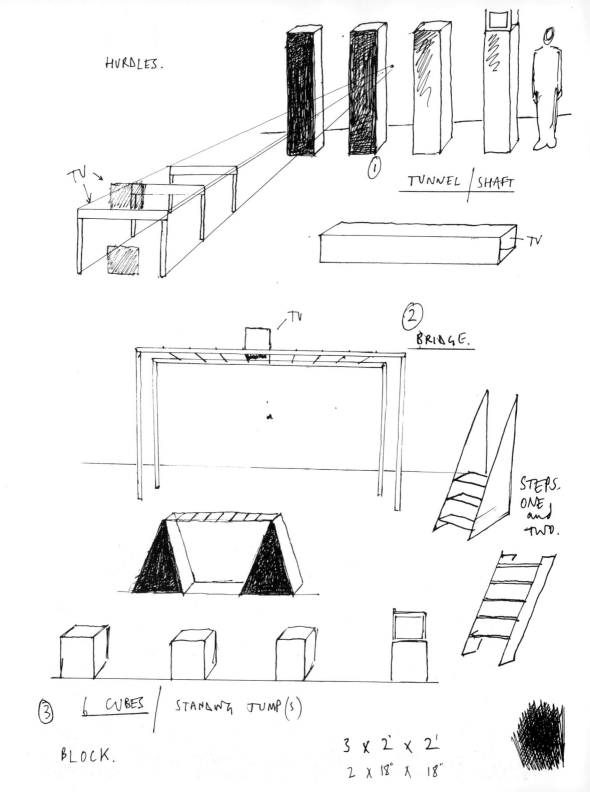

HURDLES.

TV

① TUNNEL / SHAFT

TV

TV

② BRIDGE.

STEPS.
ONE
and
TWO.

③ CUBES / STANDING JUMP(S)

BLOCK.

3 X 2' X 2'
2 X 18" X 18"

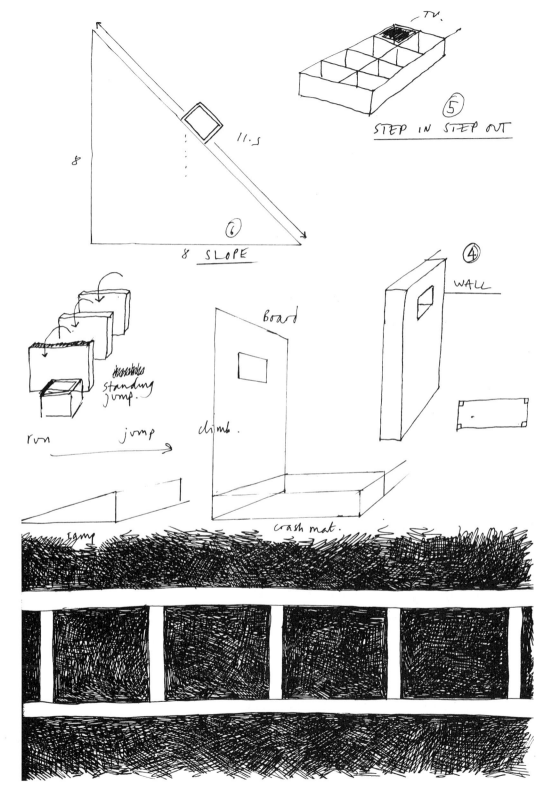

TV.

⑤

STEP IN STEP OUT

8

11.5

⑥

8 SLOPE

④

WALL

Board

shackles
standing
jump.

run   jump

climb.

crash mat.

grass

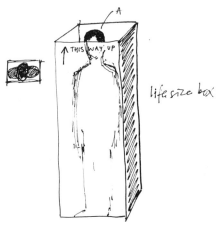

life size box

A climbs out of case.
climbs into case

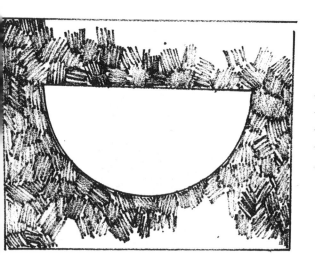

36° slope. (41° ~~±~~ slope)

Headstand
Back to front
- Slope
handstand
Bridge
falling down board!
- head over heels
Up
Heavyweight (tilt)
free fall

38°

Proposal
(4 Page diagrams)

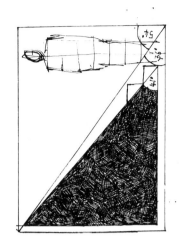

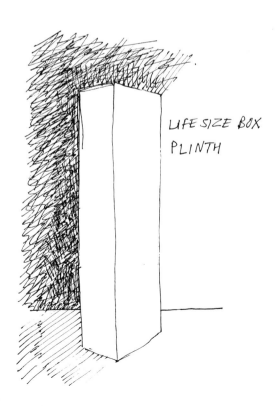

LIFE SIZE BOX
PLINTH

PLINTH

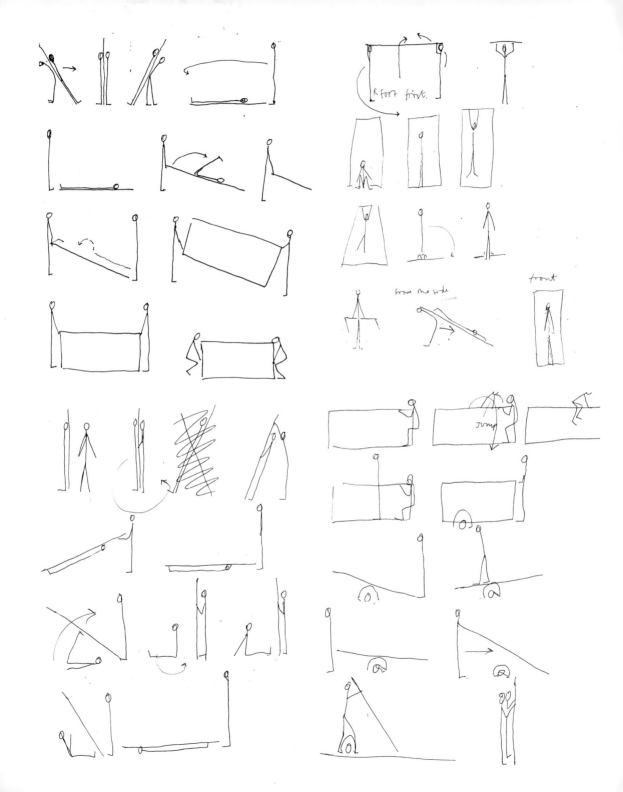

R foot first.

from the side

front

jump

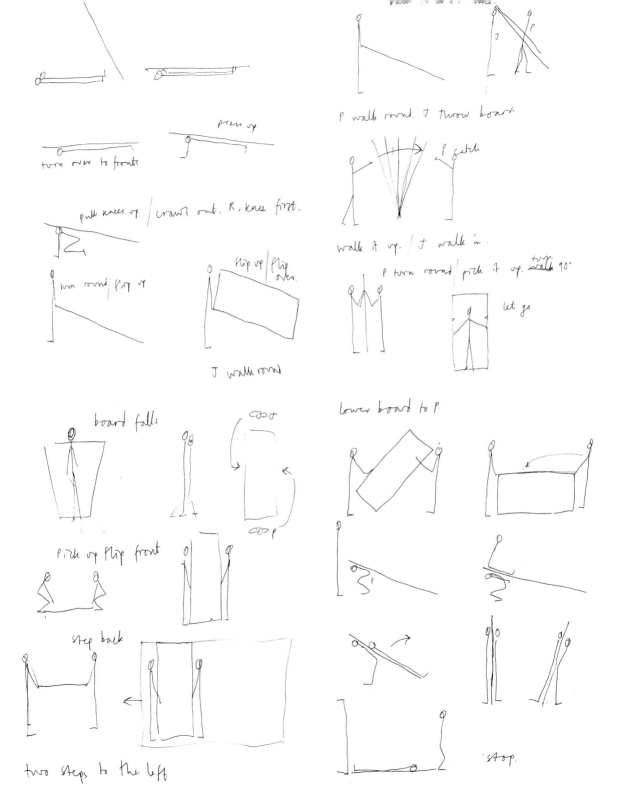

press up

turn over to front.

pull knees up / crawl out. R. knee first.

turn round / flip up

flip up / flip over.

J walks round

board falls

Pick up flip front

step back

two steps to the left

P walk round. J throw board

P catch

walk it up. / J walk in.

P turn round / pick it up. turn / walk 90°

let go

lower board to P.

stop.

lists

EXHIBITIONS

2000   'The British Art Show 5', Edinburgh, Southampton, Cardiff, Birmingham
        'Cartography', Worcester City Museum and Art Gallery; Quay Arts, Newport,
        Isle of Wight; Spike Island, Bristol
        'Let's Go To Work', Marcel Sitcoske Gallery, San Francisco
1999   'Obstacle Course and other works', First Site/The Minories, Colchester;
        John Hansard Gallery, Southampton; Mead Gallery, University of Warwick
        'This Other World of Ours', TV Gallery, Moscow
        'Triple X', Amsterdam
        'Physical Evidence', Kettle's Yard, Cambridge; Djangoly Gallery, Nottingham
        'New Video from Great Britain', Sala Mendoza, Caracas; Museo Carillo Gil,
        México City; Contemporary Art Museum, Honolulu; Museo de Bellas Artes,
        Buenos Aires
1998   'Let's Play Risk', Juice, London
        'Artimia', Dunaujvaros
        'Partners', Philadelphia Museum of Art, Philadelphia
1997   'New Video from Great Britain', Museum of Modern Art, New York
        'Bittersweet', Whitworth Gallery, Manchester
        'Video Positive', Bluecoat Gallery, Liverpool
        'Konstbrus', Sodertalje Konsthall, Sweden
1996   'Selected Works', Crawford Art Gallery, Cork
        'Electronic Undercurrents', Royal Museum of Fine Arts, Copenhagen
        'Cell 2', Barbican Centre, London
        'Instant', Camden Arts Centre, London; Tramway, Glasgow
1995   'Composite', Arnolfini, Bristol
        'Sixth Mostyn Open', Oriel Mostyn Gallery, Llandudno
1994   'East', Norwich Gallery

SELECTED SCREENINGS

2000   'Performing Bodies', Tate Modern, London
        'Stuttgart Filmwinter', Stuttgart
1999   'Recontres Video Art Plastique', Herouville St-Clair
        'Fourth Wall', Royal National Theatre, London
        Oberhausen Short Film Festival, Oberhausen
        'European Media Art Festival', Osnabrück
1998   'Performing Buildings', Tate Gallery (Bankside), London
        Architectural Association, London
        Dot Gallery, Barcelona
        'Pandaemonium', Lux Centre, London
        'Viper Festival', Lucerne (prize winner)
        'Impakt', Utrecht
        'Body Electric', Lux Cinema, London

1997   'Montréal Festival of Cinema and New Media',
        Montréal
        '7th International Video Week', Geneva
1996   'Flights of Fancy', Anthology Film Archive, New
        York
        'Videofest 96', Berlin
        'Pandaemonium', ICA, London
1995   '29th New York Expo', New York
        'European Media Art Festival', Osnabrück
        'Video Creation Festival', Alicante

BROADCASTS
1999   'Harry Houdini', Channel 4 (UK)
1998   Selected tapes, ARTE (France)
1997   'Device', BBC2 (UK)
        Selected tapes, 3SAT (Germany)
1996   'Boat', TVE (Spain)

GRANTS AND COMMISSIONS
2000   West Midlands Arts, Creative Ambition Award
        Southwest Arts, Commissions Fund
1998   'Flood', Worcester City Council Commission
        West Midlands Arts New Work and Commissions
        Award
        ARTIMIA Commission and Residency (Hungary)
1997   West Midlands Arts Film and Video Production
        Award
        South West Media Development Agency Production
        Award
        European Media Arts Residency Exchange
        (Germany)
1996   Expanding Pictures, BBC2 and Arts Council
        Broadcast Commission
1995   West Midlands Arts Bursary Award (Film and
        Video)
1994   South West Arts Film and Video Production Award